Crafting Impactful Online Courses

The Educator's Handbook for Successful Online Courses

Micheal L. Stokes

Table of Contents

Introduction

Chapter 1: The Power of Online Courses

Chapter 2: Unleashing Your Inner Expert

Chapter 3: Defining Your Course Goals

Chapter 4: Planning Your Course Content

Chapter 5: Choosing the Right Technology

Chapter 6: Strategies for Engaging Online Learners

Chapter 7: Assessing and Improving Your Online Course

Chapter 8: Scaling and Innovating Your Online Course

Chapter 9: Ensuring Learner Success in Your Online Course

Chapter 10: Leaving a Lasting Impact: The Transformative Power of Your Online Course

Chapter 11: Adapting to the Future: Trends and Strategies in Online Education

Chapter 12: Beyond the Virtual Classroom: Building a Sustainable Online Education Ecosystem

Conclusion

Introduction

Welcome to a transformative journey—a journey that delves into the heart of online education, unlocking the secrets to crafting world-class courses that resonate with learners, foster a sense of community, and leave an indelible impact on the educational landscape. As we embark on this exploration, allow me to introduce myself, the author, and provide you with a glimpse of what awaits within the pages of this comprehensive guide.

Meet the Author
Hello, I'm Micheal L. Stokes, an educator, innovator, and passionate advocate for the power of education to shape lives and communities. With 7 years of experience in both traditional and online education, I've witnessed the transformative potential of well-crafted courses that go beyond disseminating information—they inspire, empower, and cultivate a love for lifelong learning.

My journey began in Bloomington, Indiana. where I discovered my love for teaching and the profound impact a dedicated educator can have on the lives of learners. As technology transformed the educational landscape, I embraced the opportunities it presented. I've navigated the challenges, celebrated the successes, and continually sought ways to enhance the online learning experience for both educators and learners.

Through my experiences, I've come to understand that each educator possesses a unique expertise—an "expert within." This book is born from the belief that every educator has the potential to create courses that not only impart knowledge but also unleash the transformative educator within them. Whether you're an experienced online instructor or taking your first steps into the world of online education, this guide is crafted to empower you to discover, develop, and deploy your expertise in the digital realm.

What Can You Gain from This Book?

1. Comprehensive Course Creation Insights:
Why it Matters: Creating an effective online course goes beyond transferring information. It involves understanding the nuances of digital learning environments, crafting engaging content, and fostering a positive online community.
What You'll Learn: This book provides a step-by-step guide to essential elements of course creation, from defining your course objectives to incorporating multimedia elements that captivate learners.

2. Effective Communication Strategies:
Why it Matters: In the absence of a physical classroom, effective communication becomes the cornerstone of successful online teaching. Learners need clear

instructions, regular engagement, and a sense of the instructor's presence to thrive in a digital learning environment.

What You'll Learn: Discover strategies to enhance your communication skills, create instructional designs that facilitate seamless learning, and establish a strong presence that resonates with your learners.

3. Building a Strong Brand and Presence:

Why it Matters: In a vast sea of online courses, creating a strong brand identity is crucial. It's not just about what you teach; it's about how you position yourself, market your course, and build a community around your expertise.

What You'll Learn: Uncover the secrets of effective branding, positioning, and marketing for your online course. Learn how to stand out in a crowded market and build a lasting presence that attracts and retains learners.

4. Scaling Impact and Generating Passive Income:

Why it Matters: As an educator, your impact extends beyond individual courses. Scaling your impact allows you to reach a broader audience while generating passive income creates sustainability and financial freedom.

What You'll Learn: Explore strategies to scale your impact, diversify your revenue streams, and create a sustainable model for your online education endeavors.

5. Unleashing the Educator Within:

Why it Matters: Recognizing and embracing your expertise is the key to creating courses that resonate authentically with learners. Overcoming challenges, cultivating resilience, and tapping into your unique strengths are crucial aspects of unleashing the educator within you.

What You'll Learn: Discover how to navigate challenges, overcome imposter syndrome, and leverage your expertise to create courses that reflect your passion and leave a lasting impact on learners.

6. Ensuring Learner Success:

Why it Matters: Learner success is the ultimate measure of the effectiveness of your course. Fostering a positive learning culture, providing robust support systems, and addressing the diverse needs of learners contribute to their overall success.

What You'll Learn: Dive into strategies for creating a positive online learning environment, offering comprehensive learner support, and adapting your course to cater to a diverse audience.

7. Navigating Challenges and Overcoming Obstacles:

Why it Matters: The digital landscape comes with its unique set of challenges—from technical issues to maintaining learner engagement. Navigating these challenges with resilience and effective solutions is essential for a successful online teaching journey.

What You'll Learn: Equip yourself with comprehensive troubleshooting guides, transparent communication strategies, and effective solutions to overcome obstacles and create a seamless learning experience.

8. Monitoring and Celebrating Progress:

Why it Matters: Learners thrive when their achievements are acknowledged, and progress is celebrated. Implementing recognition milestones, learner showcases, and effective feedback mechanisms contribute to a positive learning experience.

What You'll Learn: Explore ways to monitor learner progress, implement milestone recognitions, and showcase exceptional learner work to create a culture of achievement and motivation.

9. Leaving a Lasting Impact:

Why it Matters: Your role as an educator extends beyond the confines of a course. Creating a legacy through education involves practical applications, alumni engagement, and fostering a community of lifelong learners.

What You'll Learn: Discover strategies for leaving a lasting impact, reflecting on transformative experiences, and building a community that extends beyond the duration of your courses.

10. Adapting to the Future:

Why it Matters: The future of online education is dynamic and ever-evolving. Staying abreast of current trends, embracing technology, and adapting your teaching strategies are crucial for continued success in the digital realm.

What You'll Learn: Explore current trends in online education, understand the strategies for adaptation, and position yourself as an innovative educator prepared for the future.

11. Building a Sustainable Ecosystem:
Why it Matters: Creating a sustainable online education ecosystem involves continuous learning opportunities, community engagement, and collaboration with industry partners. It's about fostering an environment where learners thrive and educators contribute to a broader educational landscape.
What You'll Learn: Gain insights into building a sustainable ecosystem, offering diverse learning opportunities, engaging with your community, and collaborating with industry partners for course relevance.

Why Read This Book?
As you navigate through these chapters, you'll find a wealth of practical insights, actionable strategies, and real-world examples that bring each concept to life. This isn't just a guide; it's a companion on your journey as an educator. Whether you're creating your first online course or seeking to enhance your existing ones, this book is crafted to be your go-to resource—a roadmap that navigates the complexities of online education with clarity and purpose.

By the end of this book, you'll not only have the tools and strategies to create world-class online courses but also the confidence to embrace your role as an educator who leaves a lasting impact on learners and contributes to the evolving landscape of education. The transformative power of education is in your hands—let's unleash the educator within and embark on this enrich

Chapter 1: The Power of Online Courses

In the ever-evolving landscape of education, the emergence of online courses has heralded a paradigm shift, breaking down geographical barriers and democratizing knowledge. Chapter 1 sets the stage for our exploration, delving into the profound impact and transformative power that online courses wield in the modern world.

Understanding the Evolution of Education
The traditional classroom, with its physical confines and limited reach, is giving way to a virtual realm where learning knows no boundaries. Online courses have become the linchpin of this educational evolution, offering unprecedented opportunities for both educators and learners.

Breaking Geographical Barriers
Online courses transcend the limitations of location, bringing education to the farthest corners of the globe. No longer bound by the constraints of a physical classroom, learners can access high-quality content from the comfort of their homes, fostering a global community of knowledge seekers.

Democratizing Knowledge Access
Education is no longer a privilege confined to the elite.
The power of online courses lies in their ability to
democratize knowledge, making it accessible to
individuals from diverse backgrounds. Whether you're
in a bustling metropolis or a remote village, the internet
becomes the great equalizer, providing a gateway to
education for all.

Recognizing the Opportunities for Individuals and
Businesses
The opportunities presented by online courses are as
vast as the digital landscape itself. Chapter 1 explores
how these courses have become not only a means of
personal growth but also a strategic asset for businesses
and entrepreneurs.

Empowering Individuals
For individuals, the ability to engage in online learning
opens doors to continuous personal and professional
development. Whether you're honing a new skill,
pursuing a passion, or seeking to advance your career,
online courses offer a flexible and tailored approach to
learning that adapts to your schedule and needs.

Strategic Asset for Businesses
Businesses, too, have recognized the potential of online
courses as a powerful tool for employee training and
development. Beyond internal training, creating courses
can position businesses as industry leaders, fostering
brand loyalty and trust. As the world becomes

increasingly digital, having a robust online presence through educational content is not just an option but a strategic necessity.

Navigating the Impact on Traditional Education

As online courses continue to redefine the educational landscape, questions arise about their relationship with traditional education models. This chapter addresses the coexistence and synergy between online courses and traditional methods.

Complementing Traditional Education

Online courses are not meant to replace traditional education but rather to complement it. They offer a flexible and supplementary avenue for learning, catering to diverse learning styles and preferences. Educational institutions are now incorporating online components into their curricula to enhance the overall learning experience.

Lifelong Learning and Skill Adaptability

The rapid pace of technological advancement demands continuous learning and adaptability. Online courses empower individuals to engage in lifelong learning, acquiring new skills and staying relevant in a dynamic job market. The ability to update and expand one's skill set becomes a cornerstone for success in the digital age.

Realizing the Transformative Potential

The transformative potential of online courses extends beyond the individual and organizational levels. Chapter

1 delves into the societal impact, illustrating how online education contributes to broader social and economic transformations.

Bridging Socioeconomic Gaps
Online courses act as bridges, spanning socioeconomic gaps by providing affordable and accessible education. This inclusivity ensures that individuals from various economic backgrounds can equip themselves with the knowledge and skills needed to break the cycle of poverty and contribute meaningfully to society.

Fueling Innovation and Entrepreneurship
The democratization of knowledge fuels innovation and entrepreneurship. Online courses empower aspiring entrepreneurs to acquire the necessary skills and knowledge to bring their ideas to fruition. The result is a vibrant ecosystem of innovators and creators, driving economic growth and technological advancement.

Case Studies: Inspiring Stories of Transformation
To underscore the real-world impact of online courses, Chapter 1 features inspiring case studies of individuals and businesses that have leveraged online education to achieve remarkable success.

From Novice to Expert: The Journey of an Online Learner
Explore the story of a novice learner who, armed with determination and online courses, transformed into an industry expert. This narrative highlights the personal

and professional growth made possible through the flexibility and accessibility of online learning.

Business Breakthroughs: Leveraging Online Courses for Success
Discover how businesses, both small startups and established enterprises, strategically used online courses to train their workforce, enhance their brand presence, and unlock new revenue streams.

Chapter 2: Unleashing Your Inner Expert

Let's embark on a transformative path that transcends self-doubt and imposter syndrome, paving the way for you to become a guiding light in your chosen field.

Recognizing Your Unique Expertise
Everyone possesses a reservoir of knowledge and skills that make them unique. In this section, we'll delve into the process of recognizing and appreciating your distinct expertise, whether it's honed through formal education, life experiences, or a combination of both.

Reflection and Self-Discovery
Start by reflecting on your journey so far. What experiences have shaped your skills? What knowledge have you accumulated? By recognizing and acknowledging your unique experiences, you'll uncover the expertise that sets you apart.

Identifying Passion and Strengths
Passion is often intertwined with expertise. Identify the subjects or activities that light a spark in you. Your passions are not only indicators of your expertise but also sources of inspiration for creating engaging and impactful online courses.

Building Confidence in Your Knowledge
Confidence is the cornerstone of effective teaching. This section provides practical strategies to build confidence in your knowledge and communicate it with authority.

Continual Learning and Growth Mindset
Embrace a growth mindset that sees challenges as opportunities for learning. Adopting a continual learning approach not only deepens your expertise but also demonstrates to your audience that you are committed to staying at the forefront of your field.

Validation through Teaching and Sharing
Teaching is a powerful tool for reinforcing your own knowledge. Whether through workshops, blog posts, or informal discussions, actively sharing your expertise not only validates your knowledge but also hones your ability to articulate complex concepts.

Confronting Imposter Syndrome
Imposter syndrome, the feeling of inadequacy despite evidence of competence, can be a significant barrier. This section provides strategies to confront and overcome imposter syndrome.

Acknowledging and Normalizing
Recognize that imposter syndrome is a common experience, even among accomplished individuals. By acknowledging and normalizing these feelings, you can

begin to separate self-doubt from the reality of your expertise.

Celebrating Achievements

Take stock of your achievements, no matter how small. Celebrating milestones reinforces your competence and helps counteract imposter syndrome. Keep a record of positive feedback, completed projects, and personal growth.

Embracing Your Unique Voice and Perspective

Your voice and perspective are what make your teaching style compelling. This section explores how to embrace your authenticity and infuse it into your online courses.

Authenticity as a Teaching Tool

Authenticity fosters connection. Share personal anecdotes, failures, and triumphs related to your expertise. Your authenticity will resonate with learners and create a more engaging and relatable learning experience.

Tailoring Content to Your Style

Consider your preferred teaching style – whether it's conversational, formal, or interactive. Tailor your content to align with your style, creating a cohesive and enjoyable learning environment for your audience.

Navigating Ethical Considerations

Expertise comes with a responsibility to uphold ethical standards. This section discusses the importance of integrity and ethical considerations when sharing your knowledge.

Transparency and Honesty
Be transparent about your expertise, qualifications, and any limitations you may have. Honesty fosters trust, and learners appreciate educators who are open about their expertise and its boundaries.

Respecting Diverse Perspectives
Recognize the diversity of your audience and be mindful of varying perspectives. Create an inclusive learning environment by respecting different experiences and viewpoints, fostering a community of mutual respect and understanding.

Your Expertise Unleashed

As we conclude this chapter, remember that expertise is not a static destination but a dynamic journey of continual learning and growth. You've begun the process of unleashing your inner expert, recognizing the unique value you bring to the table.

The expertise within you is a powerful force waiting to be harnessed and shared. In the subsequent chapters, we'll channel this newfound confidence and knowledge into the creation of a world-class online course. So, stand tall, embrace your expertise, and get ready to illuminate the path for learners eager to benefit from your unique insights and knowledge.

Chapter 3: Defining Your Course Goals

Defining your course goals is the compass that guides your content creation, audience engagement, and the overall impact of your course. In this chapter, we will explore the process of goal-setting, understanding the needs of your target audience, and aligning your objectives with the outcomes your learners seek.

Understanding the Significance of Clear Course Goals
Before delving into the practical aspects of goal-setting, it's crucial to comprehend why clear course goals are the linchpin of a successful online learning experience.

Guiding the Learning Path
Clear goals act as beacons, guiding both you as the educator and your learners along a structured learning path. They provide a roadmap, ensuring that every module, lesson, and activity contributes cohesively to the overall educational journey.

Fostering Learner Motivation
Goals provide learners with a sense of purpose and motivation. When students understand what they will achieve by the end of the course, they are more likely to

stay engaged, complete assignments, and actively participate in discussions.

Identifying Your Target Audience

To set effective goals, you must intimately understand the needs and aspirations of your target audience. This section guides you through the process of identifying and empathizing with your learners.

Conducting Audience Research

Invest time in researching your target audience. What are their demographics? What are their pain points, challenges, and aspirations? By gathering this information, you can tailor your course goals to directly address the specific needs of your learners.

Creating Learner Personas

Developing learner personas can be a powerful tool. Construct fictional characters that represent different segments of your audience, complete with their goals, preferences, and challenges. This exercise humanizes your audience and aids in setting goals that resonate on a personal level.

Aligning Goals with Learner Outcomes

Setting goals is not a one-size-fits-all endeavor. This section explores the art of aligning your course goals with the desired outcomes your learners seek to achieve.

Defining Clear Learning Outcomes

Begin by clearly defining the learning outcomes you want your students to attain. These outcomes should be specific, measurable, achievable, relevant, and time-bound (SMART), providing a framework for crafting precise goals.

Mapping Goals to Real-World Applications
Ensure that your goals have real-world applications. How will the knowledge gained in your course benefit learners in their personal or professional lives? By establishing practical connections, you enhance the perceived value of your course.

Crafting Goals for Different Learning Styles
Recognizing the diversity in learning styles is essential for creating inclusive and effective goals. This section explores strategies to cater to various preferences.

Visual Learners
For visual learners, goals can be supported by infographics, charts, and visually engaging materials. Clearly articulate how visual content will contribute to achieving specific objectives.

Auditory Learners
Auditory learners may benefit from goals framed in podcast-style narratives or accompanied by audio explanations. Consider how verbal instructions and discussions will aid in reaching the desired outcomes.

Kinesthetic Learners

Kinesthetic learners thrive on hands-on experiences. Goals for these learners may involve practical exercises, simulations, or interactive activities that allow them to apply theoretical concepts.

Iterative Goal Refinement
Setting goals is not a one-and-done task; it's an iterative process that evolves with ongoing feedback and assessment. This section explores the importance of refining goals based on learner progress and engagement.

Collecting and Analyzing Feedback
Actively solicit feedback from your learners. What aspects of the course are resonating with them, and where do they see room for improvement? Analyzing this feedback allows you to adjust goals to better meet the evolving needs of your audience.

Assessing Learner Progress
Regularly assess learner progress against the established goals. Are students achieving the expected outcomes, or are there areas that require additional attention? This ongoing assessment informs the refinement of goals to ensure they remain relevant and achievable.

Goals as Catalysts for Success
As we conclude this chapter, recognize the pivotal role that clear goals play in the success of your online course. These goals are not just statements; they are catalysts that propel learners toward meaningful outcomes.

Armed with a deep understanding of your audience and a commitment to iterative refinement, you are now prepared to define course goals that will shape a transformative learning experience for your students.

In the subsequent chapters, we will channel these goals into tangible content creation strategies, ensuring that every module and lesson aligns seamlessly with the overarching objectives. So, with goals as your guiding stars, let's continue our journey towards creating a world-class online course that leaves a lasting impact on your learners.

Chapter 4: Planning Your Course Content

Crafting a Comprehensive Course Outline
The course outline is the blueprint of your educational masterpiece. It provides a high-level view of the entire learning experience, offering both you and your learners a roadmap for the exciting journey ahead.

Establishing Clear Module Objectives
Begin by defining the objectives for each module. What key concepts or skills will learners gain from each module? Clarifying these objectives sets the stage for focused content creation and helps learners understand the purpose of each section.

Sequencing Modules for Progression
Consider the logical progression of modules. Should they follow a chronological order, build on increasing levels of complexity, or present interconnected themes? Sequencing modules thoughtfully ensures a smooth and intuitive learning experience.

Balancing Depth and Breadth
Strike a balance between depth and breadth in your content. While it's important to cover key topics comprehensively, be mindful not to overwhelm learners

with an excess of information. Aim for a depth of understanding that fosters mastery.

Structuring Engaging Modules and Lessons
With your course outline as a guide, let's explore how to structure individual modules and lessons to optimize engagement and comprehension.

Introduction to Each Module
Commence each module with a compelling introduction. Clearly articulate what learners will achieve in the module, why it's crucial, and how it connects to the overall course goals. An engaging start sets the tone for a positive learning experience.

Dividing Content into Digestible Lessons
Break down module content into digestible lessons. Each lesson should focus on a specific sub-topic or skill, allowing learners to absorb information in manageable chunks. This approach enhances understanding and retention.

Incorporating Varied Learning Activities
Diversify the learning experience by incorporating various activities. Blend traditional methods like readings and lectures with interactive elements such as quizzes, discussions, and hands-on exercises. This variety caters to different learning styles and keeps learners engaged.

Incorporating Engaging Multimedia Elements

Multimedia elements add a dynamic layer to your course, transforming it from a static experience to an interactive and visually stimulating journey.

Integrating Videos for Visual Appeal
Videos are powerful tools for conveying information with visual and auditory impact. Consider creating instructional videos, demonstrations, or interviews that complement textual content. Visual learners, in particular, benefit significantly from well-crafted videos.

Leveraging Infographics for Clarity
Infographics distill complex information into visually appealing and easily understandable graphics. Use infographics to illustrate processes, timelines, or key concepts, enhancing clarity and retention for learners.

Utilizing Audio for Accessibility
Audio elements, such as podcasts or recorded explanations, cater to auditory learners. Including alternative audio options alongside written content ensures a more inclusive learning experience for individuals with varying preferences.

Maintaining Consistent Branding
Consistent branding contributes to a professional and cohesive learning environment. Your course is not just a collection of lessons; it's a brand that reflects your expertise. Consider:

Visual Elements: Use a consistent color scheme, fonts, and graphics throughout your course materials.

Branded Materials: Design templates for presentations, worksheets, or any downloadable materials to maintain a polished and professional look.

Adapting Content for Diverse Learners
Recognize that your audience may consist of diverse learners with varying backgrounds, experiences, and learning needs.

Providing Multiple Learning Paths
Offer flexibility by allowing learners to choose different paths through the content. For example, provide additional resources or advanced challenges for those who want to delve deeper, while ensuring foundational material remains accessible for everyone.

Offering Translations or Subtitles
Enhance accessibility by providing translations or subtitles. This accommodates learners who may prefer or require content in languages other than the primary language of instruction.

Planning for Accessibility
Creating an accessible learning environment ensures that all learners, including those with disabilities, can fully engage with your content.

Alt Text for Images

Include descriptive alt text for images. This practice not only benefits learners with visual impairments but also improves search engine optimization (SEO) for your course materials.

Closed Captions for Videos
If your course includes videos, provide closed captions. This enhances accessibility for individuals with hearing impairments and also aids learners who may benefit from reading along with the spoken content.

Iterative Review and Enhancement
The creation of course content is an iterative process. Regularly review and enhance your materials based on learner feedback and evolving educational trends.

Gathering Learner Feedback
Actively seek feedback from learners at various stages of the course. What elements are resonating with them? Where do they find challenges? Use this valuable input to refine and enhance your content continually.

Staying Informed on Educational Trends
Stay abreast of evolving educational trends and technology. Incorporate new insights, tools, or methodologies that align with the needs and expectations of your learners.

As we conclude this chapter, recognize that your course content is more than information; it's a crafted masterpiece that shapes the learning journey for your audience. By strategically planning and incorporating engaging elements, you are not just delivering lessons; you are creating an experience that resonates with learners and fosters meaningful understanding.

In the upcoming chapters, we will continue to refine and enhance your course, channeling the creativity and structure you've applied to your content into strategies for engagement, interaction, and impact. So, let your content be the beacon that guides learners through an enriching educational experience, and let the creation of your online course be a journey filled with innovation and inspiration.

Chapter 5: Choosing the Right Technology

The choices you make in this realm can significantly impact the user experience, accessibility, and overall success of your educational venture. In this chapter, we'll explore various aspects of technology selection, from platforms and Learning Management Systems (LMS) to tools for content creation and delivery, ensuring a seamless and effective learning environment for your audience.

Exploring Platforms and Learning Management Systems (LMS)
Selecting the right platform and Learning Management System is foundational to the success of your online course. Let's delve into the considerations and features that will guide your decision-making process.

Understanding Platform Types
Platforms come in various forms, each with its unique features and purposes.

Self-Hosted Platforms: Offer complete control over your course but require more technical expertise for setup and maintenance.

Hosted Platforms: Simplify the technical aspects, allowing you to focus on content creation. However, customization options may be limited.

Marketplace Platforms: Provide built-in audiences but often come with transaction fees and restrictions.

Assessing Learning Management Systems (LMS)
LMS is the backbone of your online course, managing content, user access, and assessments. Key considerations include:

User-Friendly Interface: An intuitive interface ensures a positive user experience for both you and your learners.

Scalability: Choose an LMS that can scale with your course as it grows in content and user base.

Mobile Accessibility: Ensure the LMS supports mobile devices for learners on the go.

Selecting Tools for Content Creation and Delivery
The tools you choose for content creation and delivery will shape the quality and engagement level of your course. Let's explore the essential tools across different content formats.

Text-Based Content Tools
Word Processors: Microsoft Word or Google Docs for creating written content.

Collaborative Writing Platforms: Platforms like Dropbox Paper or Notion for collaborative content creation.

Multimedia Content Tools
Video Creation: Tools like Camtasia, Adobe Premiere, or simpler options like Loom for creating engaging video content.

Graphic Design: Canva or Adobe Spark for creating visually appealing graphics.

Audio Editing: Audacity or GarageBand for editing and enhancing audio elements.

Interactive Content Tools
Quizzes and Assessments: Tools like Google Forms, Typeform, or dedicated quiz platforms for interactive assessments.

Discussion Forums: Forum tools integrated into your LMS or standalone platforms like Discourse for fostering community engagement.

Virtual Classroom Tools
Webinar Platforms: Zoom, Microsoft Teams, or platforms like Webex for live virtual sessions.

Screen Sharing Tools: Tools like OBS Studio for dynamic screen sharing during live sessions or recorded content.

Understanding Technical Requirements

Before committing to specific tools and platforms, it's crucial to understand the technical requirements to ensure compatibility and smooth operation.

Browser Compatibility: Verify that the chosen tools and platforms are compatible with popular browsers to accommodate diverse user preferences.

Internet Connection: Consider the internet speed requirements for both content creation and consumption, especially for live sessions.

Device Compatibility: Ensure that your chosen tools and platforms are accessible across a range of devices, including desktops, laptops, tablets, and smartphones.

Exploring Accessibility Features
Accessibility is a critical consideration to ensure your course is inclusive and reaches a diverse audience.

Screen Reader Compatibility: Ensure compatibility with screen readers for visually impaired learners.

Captioning and Transcripts: Implement captions for videos and provide transcripts for audio content to assist learners with hearing impairments.

Color Contrast: Opt for a color scheme that ensures readability for individuals with visual impairments.

Securing Your Online Course

Protecting your course content and user data is paramount. Consider these security measures:

Secure Sockets Layer (SSL): Implement SSL certificates to encrypt data transmitted between users and your website.

User Authentication: Choose an LMS that offers robust user authentication features to safeguard user accounts.

Regular Backups: Regularly back up your course content to prevent data loss due to unforeseen events.

Staying Informed about Privacy Regulations
Stay informed about privacy regulations, especially if you collect user data. Familiarize yourself with data protection laws like GDPR or other regional regulations that may apply to your audience.

Exploring Free and Open-Source Options
Consider free and open-source options, especially if you're on a budget. Platforms like Moodle (LMS) and tools like Audacity (audio editing) or GIMP (graphic design) offer powerful functionalities without requiring a financial investment.

Ensuring Customer Support and Training
Choose tools and platforms with reliable customer support and training resources. Accessibility to support can be crucial in resolving technical issues promptly and

ensuring a smooth learning experience for both you and your learners.

Integrating Technology Seamlessly
Integrating your chosen tools and platforms seamlessly is vital for a cohesive user experience. Consider:

Single Sign-On (SSO): Implement SSO functionality for easy access to multiple tools without constant logins.

Data Syncing: Ensure that data such as user progress is synchronized across various tools and platforms.

Chapter 6: Strategies for Engaging Online Learners

Building a Virtual Learning Community
Creating a sense of community is essential for online learners who may be physically distant but crave connection and support. Let's explore strategies to foster a vibrant virtual learning community.

Welcome and Orientation
Personalized Greetings: Welcome learners with personalized messages or videos to create a warm and inviting atmosphere.

Clear Orientation Materials: Provide clear and concise orientation materials that guide learners through the course structure, tools, and expectations.

Icebreaker Activities
Introduction Forums: Create forums where learners can introduce themselves, share their goals, and connect with fellow participants.

Virtual Meet-and-Greets: Organize virtual meet-and-greet sessions to facilitate real-time interactions and break the ice.

Collaboration Tools
Discussion Forums: Encourage active participation through discussion forums where learners can share thoughts, ask questions, and engage in meaningful conversations.

Collaborative Projects: Foster collaboration by assigning group projects that require learners to work together towards a common goal.

Promoting Active Participation
Engage your learners actively by implementing strategies that encourage participation and interaction.

Interactive Assessments
Quizzes and Polls: Incorporate quizzes and polls to gauge understanding and stimulate critical thinking.

Peer Reviews: Integrate peer review assignments to promote collaborative learning and provide diverse perspectives.

Live Sessions
Webinars and Q&A Sessions: Host live webinars or Q&A sessions to connect directly with learners, answer questions, and provide additional insights.

Guest Speakers: Invite guest speakers to share their expertise, adding variety and real-world relevance to your course.

Feedback Loops
Regular Feedback: Provide timely and constructive feedback on assignments, forum posts, and assessments to guide learner progress.

Surveys and Reflections: Implement surveys and reflection activities to gather insights on the learning experience and adjust course dynamics accordingly.

Enhancing Content Delivery
Optimize your content delivery methods to keep learners engaged and eager to explore the material.

Varied Multimedia Elements
Engaging Videos: Craft visually appealing and informative videos to convey key concepts and maintain learner interest.

Infographics and Visual Aids: Integrate infographics, charts, and visual aids to enhance content comprehension and retention.

Interactive Modules
Gamified Elements: Infuse gamification elements like badges, leaderboards, or challenges to make the learning experience more enjoyable.

Interactive Simulations: Incorporate interactive simulations or scenarios that allow learners to apply theoretical knowledge in practical contexts.

Adapting to Different Learning Styles
Recognize the diversity in learning styles and adapt your course to cater to various preferences.

Visual Learners
Visual Content: Prioritize visual content, including images, diagrams, and video presentations, to cater to learners who grasp information more effectively through visual stimuli.

Mind Maps: Provide mind maps or visual summaries to help visual learners organize and recall information.

Auditory Learners
Audio Materials: Offer audio materials, such as recorded explanations or podcasts, for learners who benefit from auditory learning experiences.

Discussion Opportunities: Facilitate discussions and debates where auditory learners can actively participate and learn through verbal interaction.

Kinesthetic Learners
Hands-On Activities: Include hands-on activities, simulations, or interactive exercises that allow kinesthetic learners to engage physically with the material.

Practical Applications: Emphasize the real-world applications of concepts, enabling kinesthetic learners to see the relevance of what they are learning.

Implementing Gamification Techniques

Gamification adds an element of fun and competition to the learning process, making it more enjoyable and motivating.

Points and Badges

Reward Systems: Introduce point systems or badges for completing modules, achieving high scores in assessments, or actively participating in discussions.

Leaderboards: Create leaderboards that showcase the achievements of top learners, fostering healthy competition and motivation.

Challenges and Quests

Weekly Challenges: Issue weekly challenges or quests that encourage learners to explore additional resources, interact with peers, or tackle thought-provoking problems.

Storytelling Elements: Weave storytelling elements into your course, creating a narrative that guides learners through challenges and accomplishments.

Encouraging Self-Directed Learning

Empower learners to take control of their learning journey by implementing strategies that encourage self-directed exploration.

Resource Libraries

Curated Resources: Provide curated resource libraries with additional readings, videos, and materials for learners to explore based on their interests.

Learning Paths: Offer flexible learning paths that allow learners to choose the sequence of modules or topics they want to explore.

Self-Assessment Tools
Self-Assessment Quizzes: Include self-assessment quizzes or pre-tests that help learners identify areas where they need more focus.

Reflection Journals: Encourage the use of reflection journals, where learners can track their progress, set goals, and reflect on their learning journey.

Facilitating Effective Communication
Communication is key in an online learning environment. Implement strategies to facilitate effective and meaningful communication.

Clear Communication Channels
Announcement Boards: Use announcement boards to communicate important updates, clarifications, or additional resources.

Regular Newsletters: Send regular newsletters summarizing recent activities, highlighting outstanding contributions, and providing motivational messages.

Office Hours and Support
Virtual Office Hours: Schedule virtual office hours where learners can connect with you for one-on-one discussions, clarifications, or additional support.

Peer Support Networks: Encourage the formation of peer support networks where learners can help each other, share insights, and collaborate.

Cultivating a Dynamic Learning Environment
As we conclude this chapter, remember that cultivating engagement in an online learning environment is an ongoing process that requires creativity, adaptability, and a genuine commitment to learner success. By implementing a combination of community-building strategies, interactive elements, and personalized approaches, you can create a dynamic and enriching learning experience that resonates with your audience.

In the upcoming chapters, we will continue to explore advanced strategies for refining your online course, ensuring that it not only captivates learners but also leaves a lasting impact on their personal and professional development. So, let's embark on this journey of transformative education, where engagement is not just a goal but a guiding principle for a thriving online learning community.

Chapter 7: Assessing and Improving Your Online Course

Assessment is not merely about evaluating learner performance; it's a dynamic process that informs course enhancements, ensuring that your educational offering remains relevant, effective, and aligned with your overarching goals. In this chapter, we'll explore various assessment strategies, gather learner feedback, and delve into the iterative process of refining your course based on valuable insights.

Designing Effective Assessments
Assessments serve as checkpoints to gauge learner understanding and progress. Let's explore the principles of designing effective assessments that align with your course goals.

Clear Learning Objectives
Aligned Assessments: Ensure that each assessment directly aligns with specific learning objectives. Clear alignment enhances the relevance and effectiveness of assessments.

SMART Criteria: Apply SMART criteria (Specific, Measurable, Achievable, Relevant, Time-Bound) to define precise learning objectives, providing a clear framework for assessment development.

Diverse Assessment Types
Formative Assessments: Integrate formative assessments, such as quizzes, discussions, or quick polls, to gather real-time feedback and guide learners during the learning process.

Summative Assessments: Implement summative assessments, like final exams or projects, to evaluate overall understanding and mastery of course content.

Authentic and Practical
Real-World Applications: Design assessments that mirror real-world applications, allowing learners to apply theoretical knowledge to practical scenarios.

Case Studies and Projects: Incorporate case studies, projects, or simulations that challenge learners to solve problems and demonstrate their understanding in a meaningful context.

Gathering Learner Feedback
Learner feedback is a valuable resource for understanding the strengths and weaknesses of your course. Employ various methods to gather comprehensive feedback.

Surveys and Questionnaires

Post-Module Surveys: Deploy short surveys at the end of each module to capture immediate feedback on content, difficulty level, and engagement.

Mid-Course Surveys: Conduct mid-course surveys to assess overall satisfaction, identify areas for improvement, and gather insights into the learning experience.

Discussion Forums and Focus Groups
Dedicated Feedback Forums: Create discussion forums specifically for feedback, allowing learners to share their thoughts openly and engage in constructive discussions.

Focus Group Sessions: Host virtual focus group sessions with a representative sample of learners to delve deeper into their experiences and perspectives.

One-on-One Interviews
Scheduled Interviews: Offer one-on-one interviews for learners who prefer a more personal and detailed conversation about their learning journey.

Anonymous Feedback Options: Provide anonymous feedback options to encourage honest responses, especially for sensitive or critical feedback.

Analyzing Learner Performance Data
Leverage data analytics tools integrated into your Learning Management System (LMS) to gather insights into learner performance.

Tracking Progress
Completion Rates: Monitor module and course completion rates to identify potential bottlenecks or challenging topics.

Time Spent: Analyze the average time spent on different modules to assess the complexity and engagement level of content.

Assessment Results
Individual and Aggregate Scores: Review individual learner scores and aggregate results for assessments to identify areas of strength and weakness in the course.

Question-Level Analytics: Examine question-level analytics to pinpoint specific topics or concepts that learners find challenging.

Iterative Refinement Process
Based on the insights gathered from assessments and learner feedback, embark on an iterative refinement process to enhance the overall quality and effectiveness of your online course.

Prioritizing Improvements
Identify Critical Issues: Prioritize improvements by identifying critical issues that significantly impact the learning experience or hinder achievement of learning objectives.

Alignment with Goals: Ensure that proposed improvements align with the overarching goals of the course, maintaining coherence and consistency.

Content Enhancements
Clarifications and Additional Resources: Address any confusion or gaps in understanding by providing clarifications, additional resources, or supplementary materials.

Update Outdated Content: Regularly review and update content to keep it current and relevant, especially in fast-evolving fields.

Technology and Accessibility
Technical Issue Resolutions: Swiftly address technical issues reported by learners to maintain a seamless and frustration-free learning experience.

Accessibility Improvements: Continuously work towards improving accessibility features based on learner feedback and evolving accessibility standards.

Communication and Engagement
Enhanced Communication Strategies: Revise and enhance communication strategies based on feedback, ensuring clarity in instructions, announcements, and expectations.

Interactive Elements: Introduce or refine interactive elements to boost engagement and maintain a sense of community within the course.

Implementing Continuous Professional Development
As an online educator, your own professional development is a vital component of course improvement.

Staying Informed about Educational Trends
Continuous Learning: Stay informed about emerging educational trends, instructional methodologies, and technological advancements through workshops, conferences, or online courses.

Networking with Peers: Engage with other online educators to exchange insights, share best practices, and gain diverse perspectives on effective teaching methods.

Seeking Mentorship and Feedback
Mentorship Opportunities: Seek mentorship from experienced online educators who can provide guidance, share experiences, and offer constructive feedback.

Peer Reviews: Engage in peer reviews with other educators to receive valuable feedback on your teaching style, content delivery, and course design.

A Dynamic Cycle of Improvement
In conclusion, the assessment and improvement of your online course form a dynamic and cyclical process. By

consistently gathering feedback, analyzing data, and implementing targeted refinements, you ensure that your course remains a vibrant and effective educational resource. Remember, the journey of improvement is ongoing, and each iteration brings your course closer to its full potential.

Chapter 8: Scaling and Innovating Your Online Course

Scaling involves reaching a broader audience without compromising the quality of your educational offering, while innovation fosters a dynamic and cutting-edge learning experience. In this chapter, we'll delve into strategies for expanding your course's reach, enhancing scalability, and infusing innovation to keep your educational content relevant and impactful.

Scaling Your Online Course
Scaling is about increasing the reach and impact of your course without linearly increasing resources. Let's explore strategies to scale your online course effectively.

Automating Administrative Tasks
Automated Enrollments: Implement automated enrollment processes to streamline onboarding for new learners.

Grading Automation: Utilize grading automation tools within your Learning Management System (LMS) for efficiency in assessing assignments and quizzes.

Partnering with Institutions

Collaborative Partnerships: Form partnerships with educational institutions, organizations, or businesses to offer your course as part of their curriculum or professional development programs.

White Labeling: Explore white-labeling options, allowing institutions to brand and integrate your course seamlessly into their existing programs.

Utilizing Online Marketplaces
Listing on Online Platforms: Consider listing your course on popular online education platforms to tap into their user base and benefit from their marketing reach.

Revenue Sharing Models: Explore revenue-sharing models with online marketplaces, enabling you to earn income while leveraging their platform.

Enhancing Scalability
Scalability is about designing your course in a way that it can grow without becoming unmanageable. Here are strategies to enhance the scalability of your online course.

Modular Course Design
Module Independence: Design modules to be independent yet interconnected, allowing learners to engage with specific topics without needing to follow a linear progression.

Scalable Assessments: Develop assessments that can be easily adapted and scaled to accommodate a growing number of learners.

User-Friendly Learning Paths
Personalized Learning Paths: Implement personalized learning paths that cater to diverse learner needs, allowing individuals to navigate the course in a way that suits their preferences.

Adaptive Learning Platforms: Explore adaptive learning platforms that adjust content based on individual learner progress, providing a tailored experience.

Cloud-Based Infrastructure
Cloud Hosting: Utilize cloud-based hosting services to ensure your course can handle increased traffic and accommodate a growing number of learners.

Scalable Technology Solutions: Invest in scalable technology solutions that can adapt to changes in user volume and technical requirements.

Leveraging Data Analytics for Decision-Making
Data analytics plays a pivotal role in understanding learner behavior and making informed decisions for course improvement and scalability.

Learning Analytics
User Engagement Metrics: Track user engagement metrics, such as time spent on modules, completion

rates, and interaction frequency, to identify popular content and potential areas for improvement.

Assessment Analytics: Analyze assessment data to identify patterns in learner performance and areas where additional support or clarification may be needed.

User Feedback Analytics
Sentiment Analysis: Implement sentiment analysis tools to gauge the sentiment of learner feedback, helping you understand overall satisfaction and areas of concern.

Feedback Trends: Identify trends in learner feedback over time to spot recurring issues or areas that consistently receive positive responses.

Innovating Your Online Course
Innovation is the key to keeping your course content dynamic and aligned with evolving educational trends. Let's explore strategies for infusing innovation into your online course.

Emerging Technologies
Virtual Reality (VR) and Augmented Reality (AR): Explore the integration of VR and AR to create immersive learning experiences, particularly beneficial for practical or hands-on subjects.

Artificial Intelligence (AI): Leverage AI for personalized learning experiences, adaptive assessments, and intelligent chatbots that provide immediate support.

Interactive Learning Elements
Simulations and Games: Integrate simulations and educational games that make learning interactive, engaging, and enjoyable for learners.

Interactive Webinars: Enhance live sessions with interactive features such as polls, quizzes, and breakout discussions to maintain learner engagement.

Multimedia Enhancements
360-Degree Videos: Implement 360-degree videos to provide virtual tours, demonstrations, or immersive experiences related to your course content.

Interactive Infographics: Elevate the visual appeal of your course with interactive infographics that allow learners to explore information at their own pace.

Social Learning Platforms
Community Building: Establish social learning platforms or online communities where learners can connect, collaborate, and share insights beyond the formal course structure.

Peer Learning Opportunities: Promote peer learning through discussion forums, collaborative projects, and peer review activities.

Marketing and Branding Strategies

Effectively marketing and branding your course is essential for attracting a wider audience. Let's explore strategies to boost your course visibility and appeal.

Engaging Marketing Content
Compelling Course Descriptions: Craft compelling and informative course descriptions that highlight the unique value proposition and benefits of your course.

Promotional Videos: Create engaging promotional videos that showcase key aspects of your course, including testimonials, course highlights, and the learning experience.

Search Engine Optimization (SEO)
Keyword Optimization: Optimize your course content for search engines by incorporating relevant keywords in titles, descriptions, and metadata.

Backlink Building: Build backlinks to your course content through guest posts, collaborations, and partnerships, increasing its visibility on search engines.

Social Media Presence
Strategic Social Media Use: Utilize social media platforms strategically to promote your course, share relevant content, and engage with potential learners.

Influencer Collaborations: Partner with influencers or thought leaders in your course's niche to amplify your reach and credibility.

Ensuring Sustainability
Sustainability is about maintaining the long-term viability and relevance of your course. Consider these strategies for ensuring the sustainability of your online educational venture.

Regular Content Updates
Curriculum Refresh: Regularly update your course curriculum to incorporate the latest industry trends, advancements, and best practices.

Continuous Improvement Cycle: Embed a continuous improvement cycle, where assessment data and learner feedback drive regular updates and enhancements.

Community Building for Long-Term Engagement
Alumni Networks: Establish alumni networks for your course, fostering long-term connections and providing ongoing support beyond the course duration.

Lifetime Access Options: Consider offering lifetime access options for learners, allowing them to revisit and benefit from course content over an extended period.

Diversification of Revenue Streams
Additional Offerings: Diversify your revenue streams by offering additional products or services, such as workshops, consulting, or advanced courses.

Subscription Models: Explore subscription models where learners pay a recurring fee for ongoing access to updated content, resources, and community features.

Case Studies: Successful Scaling and Innovation
Explore case studies of online courses that successfully scaled their reach and implemented innovative strategies to stay ahead in the dynamic educational landscape.

As we conclude this chapter, remember that scaling and innovating your online course are ongoing processes that require adaptability, strategic planning, and a commitment to delivering exceptional educational experiences. By leveraging technology, staying informed about emerging trends, and continuously refining your approach, you can navigate the future of online education with confidence.

Chapter 9: Ensuring Learner Success in Your Online Course

As an educator, your ultimate goal is not just to disseminate information but to guide and empower learners on their educational journey. In this chapter, we'll explore a comprehensive array of techniques, from fostering a positive online learning culture to providing robust support systems, all aimed at maximizing learner success in your online course.

Fostering a Positive Online Learning Culture
Creating a positive learning culture is foundational to learner success. It establishes an environment where learners feel motivated, supported, and eager to engage with the course content. Let's explore strategies for cultivating a positive online learning culture.

Clear Expectations and Guidelines
Transparent Communication: Clearly communicate course expectations, guidelines, and assessment criteria to avoid ambiguity and empower learners to succeed.

Orientation Materials: Provide comprehensive orientation materials that introduce learners to the course structure, learning resources, and communication channels.

Building a Supportive Community
Peer Interaction Opportunities: Foster opportunities for peer interaction through discussion forums, group projects, and collaborative activities.

Instructor Presence: Actively engage with learners through announcements, discussion participation, and personalized feedback to create a sense of instructor presence.

Encouraging Positive Communication
Constructive Feedback Norms: Establish norms for constructive feedback within the online community, emphasizing respectful and helpful communication.

Encouraging Questions: Create an environment where learners feel comfortable asking questions, seeking clarification, and engaging in discussions.

Providing Robust Support Systems
Support systems play a crucial role in addressing learner needs, doubts, and challenges. Let's explore strategies for providing robust support systems within your online course.

Responsive Communication Channels

Timely Email Responses: Set expectations for response times and consistently respond to learner emails in a timely manner, providing the support needed.

Discussion Forum Monitoring: Actively monitor and participate in discussion forums to address queries, provide additional insights, and facilitate peer-to-peer support.

Accessible Help Resources
Comprehensive FAQs: Develop a comprehensive Frequently Asked Questions (FAQs) section that addresses common queries and concerns, empowering learners to find quick answers.

Tutorial Videos: Create tutorial videos that guide learners through common technical issues, platform navigation, and other challenges they may encounter.

Personalized Support Mechanisms
Virtual Office Hours: Schedule virtual office hours for one-on-one discussions, allowing learners to seek personalized guidance on course content or address specific concerns.

Peer Mentoring Programs: Establish peer mentoring programs where experienced learners provide guidance and support to those who may be struggling.

Implementing Effective Feedback Mechanisms

Feedback is a cornerstone of the learning process, guiding learners toward improvement and mastery. Let's explore effective feedback mechanisms to enhance learner success.

Timely and Constructive Feedback
Prompt Assessment Grading: Strive to provide prompt grading for assessments, ensuring that learners receive timely feedback to inform their understanding and progress.

Constructive Critique: Offer constructive and specific feedback that highlights strengths, identifies areas for improvement, and suggests actionable steps for enhancement.

Formative Assessment Strategies
Quizzes and Polls: Integrate formative assessments like quizzes and polls throughout the course to gauge understanding in real-time and guide learners toward mastery.

Peer Review Opportunities: Incorporate peer review assignments that provide learners with diverse perspectives, fostering collaboration and improvement.

Nurturing Inclusivity and Diversity
Inclusive and diverse learning environments contribute significantly to learner success. Let's explore strategies for nurturing inclusivity and diversity within your online course.

Universal Design Principles
Accessible Course Materials: Apply universal design principles to ensure course materials are accessible to learners with diverse abilities and learning styles.

Multimodal Content: Present information in various formats, including text, audio, and visuals, to cater to different learning preferences.

Cultivating Cultural Sensitivity
Diverse Examples and References: Use diverse examples and references in course content to reflect a variety of cultural perspectives and experiences.

Sensitivity Training: Provide sensitivity training for instructors and encourage inclusive language to create a welcoming environment for all learners.

Flexible Learning Paths
Adaptable Assignments: Offer adaptable assignments that allow learners to choose topics or projects aligned with their interests or experiences.

Customizable Learning Journeys: Facilitate customizable learning paths, enabling learners to explore content in a way that resonates with their cultural background and personal context.

Empowering Self-Directed Learning

Empowering learners to take control of their learning journey fosters autonomy and a sense of ownership. Let's explore strategies for promoting self-directed learning.

Goal-Setting Exercises
Individual Learning Goals: Encourage learners to set individual learning goals at the beginning of the course, providing direction and purpose.

Reflection Journals: Integrate reflection journals where learners can periodically assess their progress, revisit goals, and adjust their learning strategies.

Resource Exploration Opportunities
Curated Resource Libraries: Create curated resource libraries that allow learners to explore additional materials based on their interests, deepening their understanding of specific topics.

Learning Paths: Implement learning paths that provide flexibility in the sequence of modules, enabling learners to navigate the course at their own pace.

Skill-building Workshops
Optional Workshops: Offer optional skill-building workshops or webinars that go beyond the core content, allowing learners to expand their knowledge in areas of interest.

Peer-Led Workshops: Facilitate peer-led workshops where advanced learners share insights, tips, and practical strategies for mastering challenging concepts.

Navigating Challenges and Overcoming Obstacles
Learners may encounter challenges or obstacles during their online learning journey. Let's explore strategies for helping learners navigate difficulties and overcome obstacles.

Comprehensive Troubleshooting Guides
Technical Issue Troubleshooting: Develop comprehensive troubleshooting guides that address common technical issues learners may encounter, empowering them to resolve problems independently.

Study Skills Resources: Provide resources on effective study skills, time management, and stress reduction to help learners overcome challenges related to organization and workload.

Transparent Communication during Difficult Times
Open Communication Channels: Maintain open communication channels during challenging times, such as technical disruptions or external factors impacting the course schedule.

Flexibility and Accommodations: Demonstrate flexibility and offer accommodations when needed, recognizing that learners may face unforeseen circumstances.

Monitoring and Celebrating Progress
Acknowledging and celebrating learner progress is
crucial for motivation and a sense of accomplishment.
Let's explore strategies for monitoring and celebrating
progress within your online course.

Milestone Recognitions
Completion Milestones: Recognize learners'
achievements by celebrating completion milestones,
whether it's finishing a module, passing an assessment,
or completing the entire course.

Digital Badges or Certificates: Issue digital badges or
certificates for specific accomplishments, providing
tangible recognition of learners' efforts and
achievements.

Learner Showcases
Showcasing Exceptional Work: Showcase exceptional
learner work through dedicated platforms, newsletters,
or virtual events, fostering a culture of excellence and
motivation.

Highlighting Success Stories: Share success stories of
learners who have applied course concepts in real-world
scenarios, inspiring others and showcasing the practical
impact of the course.

Guiding Learners to Success
In conclusion, guiding learners to success in your online
course requires a holistic approach that encompasses

positive culture, robust support systems, effective feedback mechanisms, and strategies for inclusivity and empowerment. As you continue refining your online course, remember that the success of your learners is a testament to the effectiveness of your educational efforts.

Chapter 10: Leaving a Lasting Impact: The Transformative Power of Your Online Course

Building a Legacy Through Education
As an online educator, you have the unique opportunity to leave a lasting legacy through the knowledge and skills imparted in your course. Let's explore strategies for building a legacy that extends beyond the course duration.

Focus on Practical Applications
Real-World Relevance: Emphasize the practical applications of the knowledge and skills learned in your course, empowering learners to apply what they've gained in their personal and professional lives.

Case Studies and Success Stories: Showcase real-life case studies and success stories that highlight the tangible impact of your course on individuals and their accomplishments.

Alumni Engagement and Success
Alumni Networks: Establish and maintain alumni networks, providing a platform for past learners to

connect, share experiences, and contribute to the ongoing success of the course.

Highlighting Achievements: Regularly showcase the achievements of course alumni, celebrating their career advancements, projects, or contributions to their respective fields.

Cultivating a Community of Lifelong Learners
The journey of learning doesn't end with the completion of a course; it continues throughout life. Foster a community of lifelong learners who continue to seek knowledge and growth beyond the confines of your course.

Continuous Learning Opportunities
Advanced Courses and Specializations: Offer advanced courses or specializations that cater to learners seeking to deepen their expertise in specific areas related to the original course.

Regular Updates and Additions: Provide regular updates and additions to course content to keep it current, ensuring that learners have access to the latest information in their field of study.

Networking and Collaboration
Professional Development Events: Organize virtual events, webinars, or workshops that facilitate ongoing networking and collaboration among learners, fostering a sense of community.

Collaborative Projects: Encourage learners to engage in collaborative projects or research initiatives, creating opportunities for them to work together and contribute collectively to their fields.

Reflecting on Transformative Learning Experiences
Take a moment to reflect on the transformative power of education and the role your online course plays in shaping the learning experiences of individuals.

Personal Growth Stories
Encouraging Reflective Practices: Encourage learners to engage in reflective practices, such as journaling or self-assessment, to document their personal growth and insights gained from the course.

Sharing Transformative Stories: Provide a platform for learners to share their transformative learning stories, allowing them to inspire others and contribute to the collective narrative of the course's impact.

Surveys and Feedback
Post-Course Surveys: Conduct post-course surveys to gather insights on the transformative aspects of the learning experience, including changes in mindset, skill acquisition, and personal or professional growth.

Long-Term Impact Assessments: Implement long-term impact assessments to track the sustained influence of your course on learners' lives and careers.

Nurturing a Culture of Continued Support
The journey doesn't end when learners complete the
course; it evolves into a lifelong pursuit of knowledge.
Nurture a culture of continued support to ensure
learners feel connected and supported even after the
course concludes.

Extended Support Channels
Post-Course Resources: Provide a repository of
post-course resources, including additional readings,
advanced materials, and links to relevant industry
updates.

Virtual Office Hours and Q&A Sessions: Continue
hosting virtual office hours or Q&A sessions periodically
to address questions, offer guidance, and foster an
ongoing connection with learners.

Alumni Mentorship Programs
Mentorship Opportunities: Establish alumni mentorship
programs where experienced course graduates can
mentor newer learners, creating a supportive ecosystem
of guidance and knowledge-sharing.

Skill-Exchange Platforms: Create platforms where
learners can exchange skills, experiences, and insights,
facilitating a continuous cycle of learning and
mentorship.

Reflecting on Your Journey as an Educator

Take a moment to reflect on your own journey as an educator and the impact you've had on the lives of learners.

Personal Growth and Professional Development
Continuous Educator Development: Prioritize your own continuous professional development, staying informed about educational trends, technology advancements, and innovative teaching methodologies.

Feedback and Self-Reflection: Seek feedback from learners and colleagues, engaging in regular self-reflection to identify areas for improvement and growth in your role as an educator.

Celebrating Achievements
Acknowledging Milestones: Celebrate milestones in your journey as an educator, whether it's the successful completion of a course, positive feedback from learners, or achieving personal professional development goals.

Showcasing Impact: Showcase the impact of your courses through testimonials, success stories, and tangible outcomes achieved by learners.

Leaving a Legacy of Empowerment
Ultimately, the true measure of your success as an educator lies in the empowerment of your learners. Reflect on the legacy you aim to leave—a legacy of individuals who are not only well-versed in the subject

matter but are empowered to make a positive impact on the world.

Empowering Future Leaders
Leadership Development: Foster leadership skills among learners, equipping them with the confidence and capabilities to lead initiatives, projects, or even entire teams in their respective fields.

Entrepreneurial Mindset: Encourage an entrepreneurial mindset, inspiring learners to apply creativity and innovation to solve challenges and contribute to positive change.

Global Impact
International Perspectives: Cultivate an international perspective among learners, fostering an understanding of global issues and encouraging contributions to solutions on a global scale.

Social Impact Initiatives: Support and showcase learners who initiate social impact projects or contribute to community development, emphasizing the potential for education to drive positive change.

Case Studies: Stories of Lasting Impact
Explore case studies that exemplify the lasting impact of online courses, showcasing how educators have left an indelible mark on the lives of learners.

Your Educational Legacy

As we conclude this comprehensive guide, remember that the impact of your online course extends far beyond the virtual classroom. You have the power to shape the learning journeys of individuals, inspire lifelong curiosity, and contribute to positive change in the world. The legacy you leave is not just about the knowledge transferred but the empowerment instilled in learners to navigate the complexities of their chosen paths.

Chapter 11: Adapting to the Future: Trends and Strategies in Online Education

As we navigate the ever-evolving landscape of education, it's crucial to stay ahead of the curve and adapt to emerging trends and innovations in online learning. In this chapter, we'll explore the current trends shaping the future of online education and provide strategies for educators to stay relevant, engage learners effectively, and harness the full potential of technological advancements.

Understanding Current Trends in Online Education
1. Microlearning and Modular Courses:
What is it: Microlearning involves breaking down course content into smaller, easily digestible modules.
Why it matters: Learners prefer bite-sized, focused learning experiences, allowing for flexibility and efficient knowledge acquisition.
Strategies: Design courses with short modules, incorporate multimedia elements, and provide quick assessments for immediate feedback.

2. Personalized Learning Paths:

What is it: Tailoring the learning experience to individual preferences, goals, and progress.
Why it matters: Personalization enhances engagement and caters to diverse learning styles, fostering a more effective learning environment.
Strategies: Utilize adaptive learning platforms, offer choices in assignments, and provide personalized feedback based on individual performance.

3. Collaborative and Social Learning:
What is it: Emphasizing group interactions, discussions, and collaborative projects.
Why it matters: Social learning enhances engagement, fosters a sense of community, and allows learners to benefit from diverse perspectives.
Strategies: Incorporate discussion forums, group assignments, and virtual collaboration tools to encourage interaction among learners.

4. Augmented and Virtual Reality (AR/VR):
What is it: Integration of AR and VR technologies for immersive learning experiences.
Why it matters: AR and VR enhance engagement and provide realistic simulations, particularly beneficial for hands-on or practical subjects.
Strategies: Explore AR/VR applications, create virtual labs or simulations, and leverage immersive experiences to reinforce theoretical concepts.

5. Data-Driven Decision-Making:

What is it: Using analytics and data to inform instructional design and improve learning outcomes.
Why it matters: Data-driven insights help educators understand learner behavior, identify areas for improvement, and enhance course effectiveness.
Strategies: Utilize Learning Management System (LMS) analytics, conduct regular assessments, and gather feedback to inform continuous improvement.

Strategies for Adapting to Future Trends
1. Embrace Technology Integration:
Leverage emerging technologies, such as AI, chatbots, and interactive elements, to enhance the overall learning experience.
Regularly update and optimize your course with the latest tools and features that promote engagement and interactivity.

2. Flexible and Accessible Course Design:
Design courses with flexibility in mind, accommodating various learning styles, time zones, and accessibility needs.
Provide transcripts, captions, and alternative formats for multimedia content to ensure inclusivity.

3. Continuous Professional Development:
Stay informed about the latest trends in education through workshops, conferences, and online courses.
Engage in peer learning, collaborate with other educators, and participate in communities to exchange insights and best practices.

4. Agile Course Development:
Adopt agile development principles to respond quickly to changes, update content, and address emerging needs.
Gather feedback regularly and use it to make incremental improvements to the course structure, content, and delivery.

5. Cultivate a Learning Community:
Foster a sense of community among learners by facilitating discussions, collaborative projects, and networking opportunities.
Encourage peer support and mentorship to create a supportive environment that extends beyond the confines of the course.

6. Global Perspectives and Cultural Sensitivity:
Integrate diverse examples, case studies, and references to provide a global perspective in your course.
Consider the cultural background of your learners, and ensure that your content and communication are inclusive and culturally sensitive.

7. Adaptive Assessments and Feedback:
Implement adaptive assessments that adjust difficulty based on individual learner performance.
Provide timely and constructive feedback that guides learners on their strengths, areas for improvement, and next steps in their learning journey.
The Role of Educators in the Future of Online Learning

As online education evolves, educators play a pivotal role in shaping the future of learning. Here are key responsibilities for educators in adapting to the changing landscape:

1. Facilitators of Engagement:
Actively engage learners through discussions, feedback, and interactive activities.
Foster a positive and collaborative online learning environment that motivates learners to participate and contribute.

2. Curators of Relevant Content:
Stay updated on industry trends and advancements relevant to your course content.
Curate and deliver content that is not only informative but also aligned with real-world applications and current developments.

3. Adaptive Instructors:
Embrace adaptability and flexibility in your teaching approach.
Recognize and address the diverse learning needs and preferences of your learners.

4. Data-Driven Decision-Makers:
Utilize data analytics to understand learner behavior, assess the effectiveness of your course, and make informed decisions for improvements.

Regularly review assessment results, engagement metrics, and learner feedback to refine your teaching strategies.

5. Promoters of Lifelong Learning:
Instill a passion for lifelong learning by modeling curiosity, continuous improvement, and a growth mindset.
Encourage learners to explore beyond the course content, pursue further education, and apply their knowledge in diverse contexts.

6. Catalysts for Innovation:
Embrace innovation in instructional design, technology integration, and teaching methodologies.
Act as a catalyst for positive change, inspiring learners to think creatively and adapt to evolving educational landscapes.

Navigating the Future with Confidence
As we conclude this chapter, remember that the future of online education holds endless possibilities for innovative and transformative learning experiences. By staying attuned to current trends, embracing technology, and cultivating a learner-centric approach, educators can navigate the evolving landscape with confidence. Your role as an educator extends beyond the virtual classroom—it's about empowering learners to thrive in a dynamic and ever-changing world.

Chapter 12: Beyond the Virtual Classroom: Building a Sustainable Online Education Ecosystem

As an educator, your impact can go far beyond a single class, creating a lasting legacy and contributing to the broader landscape of online education.

Understanding a Sustainable Online Education Ecosystem
A sustainable online education ecosystem is one that not only delivers quality courses but also fosters ongoing learning, community building, and collaboration. It involves creating an environment where learners, educators, and stakeholders thrive collectively. Let's delve into key elements of building such an ecosystem.

1. Continuous Learning Opportunities:
Offer a variety of courses, workshops, and resources to cater to diverse learning needs.
Implement a tiered system, providing introductory, intermediate, and advanced levels to accommodate learners at various stages of expertise.

2. Community Engagement and Networking:
Establish and nurture a vibrant online learning community where learners can connect, collaborate, and share insights.
Facilitate networking opportunities through forums, discussion groups, and virtual events, fostering a sense of belonging and collective learning.

3. Mentorship Programs:
Implement mentorship initiatives where experienced learners or alumni mentor newcomers.
Provide guidance on career development, skill enhancement, and navigating the learning journey within the online education ecosystem.

4. Resource Libraries and Knowledge Hubs:
Create centralized resource libraries containing additional readings, case studies, and multimedia content.

Develop knowledge hubs that serve as repositories for industry trends, research findings, and the latest developments in relevant fields.

5. Industry Collaboration and Partnerships:
Forge collaborations with industry partners to ensure course content remains relevant and aligned with real-world needs.
Explore opportunities for joint initiatives, guest lectures, and projects that bridge the gap between academia and industry.

Strategies for Building a Sustainable Online Education Ecosystem

1. Diversification of Course Offerings:

Expand your course portfolio to cater to a broader audience and address a range of learning objectives.
Regularly assess market trends and learner preferences to identify areas for new course development.

2. Lifelong Learning Pathways:

Design courses with clear pathways for lifelong learning, offering advanced modules or specialized tracks for continuous skill development.
Implement a credentialing system that acknowledges learners' achievements and encourages them to pursue further education within the ecosystem.

3. Gamification and Interactive Elements:

Integrate gamification elements to enhance engagement and make learning more enjoyable.
Implement interactive features such as quizzes, simulations, and virtual labs to create an immersive learning experience.

4. Robust Support and Guidance Systems:

Enhance support systems by providing accessible help resources, virtual office hours, and peer mentoring programs.
Implement AI-driven chatbots to offer immediate assistance and guidance on common queries.

5. Regular Feedback and Iterative Improvement:
Establish mechanisms for collecting regular feedback from learners and stakeholders.
Use feedback to iteratively improve courses, content delivery, and overall user experience within the online education ecosystem.

6. Global Reach and Inclusivity:
Develop strategies to reach a global audience, considering diverse cultural contexts and learning preferences.
Implement inclusive design principles to ensure accessibility for learners with varying abilities and backgrounds.

7. Sustainable Business Models:
Explore sustainable business models, such as subscription-based offerings, partnerships, or diversified revenue streams.

Consider offering scholarships or financial aid to ensure inclusivity and affordability.

1. Curriculum Innovation and Alignment:
Continuously innovate course content to align with evolving industry needs and technological advancements.
Collaborate with industry experts to ensure the curriculum remains relevant and cutting-edge.

2. Community Building and Engagement:

Actively participate in community-building efforts by moderating forums, hosting virtual events, and fostering a positive learning environment.
Encourage learners to engage with each other, share experiences, and contribute to the collective knowledge of the ecosystem.

3. Mentorship and Guidance:
Offer mentorship to learners, providing insights into career paths, industry trends, and personal development.
Collaborate with other educators to establish comprehensive mentorship programs within the ecosystem.

4. Data-Informed Decision-Making:
Utilize data analytics to understand learner behavior, assess course performance, and identify areas for improvement.
Use data to inform decisions on curriculum updates, engagement strategies, and resource allocation.

5. Professional Development Initiatives:
Engage in continuous professional development to stay abreast of educational trends, technology advancements, and pedagogical innovations.
Share knowledge with colleagues and actively contribute to the growth of the broader educator community within the ecosystem.

6. Advocacy for Inclusivity and Diversity:

Advocate for inclusivity and diversity within the online education ecosystem.
Consider diverse perspectives in course design, promote culturally sensitive content, and create an environment that values varied backgrounds and experiences.

7. Collaboration with Stakeholders:
Collaborate with industry partners, institutions, and other stakeholders to enhance the overall quality and relevance of the ecosystem.
Foster collaborative projects, research initiatives, and joint ventures that benefit learners and contribute to the ecosystem's sustainability.

A Sustainable Future of Learning
As we conclude this guide, envision a future where online education transcends traditional boundaries, creating a sustainable ecosystem that empowers learners and educators alike. Your role as an educator is not only to disseminate knowledge but to contribute to the ongoing growth and evolution of the online education landscape.

By embracing innovation, fostering community, and advocating for inclusivity, you can play a pivotal role in building a sustainable online education ecosystem. Your dedication to continuous improvement, coupled with a commitment to lifelong learning, will leave a lasting legacy that extends far beyond individual courses.

Thank you for embarking on this journey of exploration and empowerment. Here's to the educators shaping the future of online education and the learners whose lives are enriched by the knowledge and skills acquired within these virtual classrooms. May your contributions resonate in the hearts and minds of learners, fostering a culture of continuous learning and growth in the years to come.

Conclusion

Shaping a Transformative Future in Online Education

As we bring this comprehensive guide to a close, it's time to reflect on the transformative journey we've embarked on—a journey that transcends the virtual classroom and envisions a sustainable future for online education. In each chapter, we explored the intricate layers of creating, enhancing, and sustaining world-class online courses. Now, let's distill the key insights into a compelling conclusion that underscores the significance of online education in shaping a transformative future.

The Evolution of Online Education
The landscape of education has undergone a remarkable evolution, and online learning stands at the forefront of this transformative shift. No longer confined to traditional classrooms, education has become a dynamic and accessible endeavor that transcends geographical boundaries. Online education empowers learners worldwide, offering flexibility, diverse learning experiences, and the opportunity to acquire skills tailored to the demands of the ever-changing global landscape.

The Educator's Role as a Catalyst for Change

Central to this evolution is the pivotal role of educators—the architects of knowledge, the guides through digital realms, and the mentors shaping the future. As an educator, you are not just a transmitter of information but a catalyst for change, inspiring learners to explore, question, and adapt. Throughout this guide, we've explored strategies to unleash the educator within you, guiding you to create courses that resonate with learners and leave an indelible mark on their educational journey.

Empowering Learners to Unleash Their Potential
At the heart of online education is the learner—an individual seeking knowledge, skills, and personal growth. The transformative power of education lies in its ability to unlock the latent potential within each learner. By providing comprehensive and engaging online courses, educators become facilitators of transformation, empowering learners to excel, innovate, and contribute meaningfully to their chosen fields.

Crafting World-Class Online Courses: A Recap
Let's revisit the key elements we explored in crafting world-class online courses:

1. Course Creation Essentials:
Clarity of Purpose: Clearly define the purpose and objectives of your course, setting the foundation for a focused and impactful learning experience.

Engaging Content: Craft engaging content that leverages multimedia elements, interactive components, and real-world applications to captivate learners.

2. Effective Communication Strategies:
Clear Instructional Design: Implement clear and effective instructional design, ensuring seamless navigation and comprehension of course content.
Active Instructor Presence: Foster a sense of instructor presence through regular communication, personalized feedback, and active engagement with learners.

3. Building a Strong Brand and Presence:
Branding and Positioning: Develop a strong brand identity for your online course, creating a memorable and recognizable presence in the competitive online education landscape.
Marketing and Outreach: Implement effective marketing strategies to reach your target audience, utilizing various channels to promote your course and build a community of learners.

4. Scaling Impact and Generating Passive Income:
Scalability Strategies: Explore scalability options to reach a broader audience without compromising the quality of your course.
Passive Income Streams: Diversify revenue streams by incorporating passive income strategies, such as affiliate marketing, memberships, or licensing.

5. Unleashing the Educator Within:

Discovering Your Expertise: Recognize and leverage your expertise to create courses that reflect your passion and knowledge.

Overcoming Challenges: Address common challenges faced by educators, from imposter syndrome to technical hurdles, with resilience and creativity.

6. Ensuring Learner Success:
Fostering a Positive Learning Culture: Create a positive and inclusive learning environment by setting clear expectations, building a supportive community, and encouraging positive communication.

Robust Support Systems: Provide responsive communication channels, accessible help resources, and personalized support mechanisms to address learner needs effectively.

7. Navigating Challenges and Overcoming Obstacles:
Comprehensive Troubleshooting: Develop troubleshooting guides and resources to empower learners to overcome technical challenges independently.

Transparent Communication: Maintain open communication channels during challenging times, demonstrating flexibility and accommodations when needed.

8. Monitoring and Celebrating Progress:
Milestone Recognitions: Acknowledge learners' achievements with milestone recognitions, digital badges, or certificates.

Learner Showcases: Showcase exceptional learner work and success stories to inspire others and highlight the practical impact of your course.

9. Leaving a Lasting Impact:
Legacy Through Education: Build a legacy by focusing on practical applications, alumni engagement, and cultivating a community of lifelong learners.
Reflecting on Transformative Experiences: Encourage reflective practices, share personal growth stories, and implement surveys to assess the transformative impact of your course.

10. Adapting to the Future:
Understanding Current Trends: Embrace microlearning, personalized learning paths, collaborative and social learning, AR/VR technologies, and data-driven decision-making.
Strategies for Adaptation: Embrace technology integration, flexible course design, continuous professional development, agile course development, and global perspectives.

11. Building a Sustainable Ecosystem:
Continuous Learning Opportunities: Offer diverse courses and resources to cater to varied learning needs.
Community Engagement: Foster a sense of community through networking, mentorship programs, and shared knowledge hubs.

Industry Collaboration: Collaborate with industry partners to ensure course relevance and foster real-world connections.

Embracing a Transformative Future

As we conclude this guide, envision the impact your role as an educator can have on the future of online education. It's not just about creating courses; it's about shaping a transformative future where learning is accessible, engaging, and sustainable. Each course you create, each learner you empower, contributes to the collective growth of an evolving educational ecosystem.

The journey doesn't end here—it continues with each new course, each innovative adaptation to emerging trends, and each learner's success story. As an educator, you are an agent of change, a guide through the vast landscape of knowledge, and a facilitator of transformative experiences. Embrace the challenges, celebrate the victories, and remain committed to the profound impact education can have on individuals and society.

Thank you for joining us on this exploration of online education. May your journey

Appendix: Resources for Further Exploration

In this comprehensive appendix, we've curated a wealth of resources to support your continued exploration and mastery of the world of online education. Whether you're an aspiring course creator, an experienced educator, or a lifelong learner, these tools, platforms, and references will enhance your understanding and effectiveness in the evolving landscape of online learning.

Online Course Creation Platforms:
Udemy: A leading online learning platform that allows educators to create and sell courses on a wide range of topics.

Website: Udemy
Coursera: A platform offering online courses, specializations, and degrees in collaboration with top universities and organizations.

Website: Coursera
Teachable: A user-friendly platform for creating and selling online courses with customizable features.

Website: Teachable
edX: A platform offering online courses and degrees from universities and institutions worldwide.

Website: edX
Learning Management Systems (LMS):
Moodle: An open-source LMS designed for educators to create and manage online courses.

Website: Moodle
Canvas by Instructure: A cloud-based LMS with features for course creation, collaboration, and assessment.

Website: Canvas
Blackboard Learn: A comprehensive LMS with tools for
content creation, collaboration, and student
engagement.

Website: Blackboard Learn
Multimedia Creation Tools:
Camtasia: A versatile tool for screen recording, video
editing, and creating multimedia content for online
courses.

Website: Camtasia
Canva: A graphic design platform with easy-to-use tools
for creating visual content, presentations, and course
materials.

Website: Canva
Audacity: An open-source audio editing software for
recording and editing podcast-style content.

Website: Audacity
Educational Technology and Trends:
EdSurge: A comprehensive resource for news, analysis,
and insights on educational technology and trends.

Website: EdSurge
Educause Review: A publication providing articles,
research, and thought leadership on higher education
and technology.

Website: Educause Review
eLearning Industry: An online community with articles, reviews, and resources on eLearning and educational technology.

Website: eLearning Industry
Professional Development and Communities:
LinkedIn Learning: An online platform offering a wide range of courses for professional development and skill enhancement.

Website: LinkedIn Learning
Higher Ed Learning Collective: A community of higher education professionals sharing resources and insights.

Website: Higher Ed Learning Collective
Edutopia: A resource from the George Lucas Educational Foundation, providing articles, videos, and insights on innovative teaching practices.

Website: Edutopia
Research and Publications:
Journal of Online Learning and Teaching (JOLT): An open-access journal focusing on research in online learning and teaching.

Website: JOLT
The Chronicle of Higher Education: A publication covering news, insights, and analysis on higher education.

Website: Chronicle of Higher Education
International Review of Research in Open and
Distributed Learning (IRRODL): An open-access journal
publishing research on open and distributed learning.

Website: IRRODL
Additional Resources:
Quality Matters: An organization providing quality
assurance in online learning through research-backed
standards and tools.

Website: Quality Matters
Open Educational Resources (OER) Commons: A
platform offering a vast collection of open educational
resources for educators and learners.

Website: OER Commons
Creative Commons: A licensing system allowing creators
to share their work with flexible usage permissions.

Website: Creative Commons
Feel free to explore these resources to enhance your
expertise, stay informed about industry trends, and
continue your journey as a trailblazer in online
education. As the landscape evolves, your commitment
to learning and adapting will ensure that your courses
remain impactful and relevant in the ever-changing
world of education. Happy learning!